ISAAC ASIMOV'S NEW LIBRARY OF THE UNIVERSE

MYSTERIES OF DEEP SPACE:
BLACK HOLES, PULSARS, AND QUASARS

BY ISAAC ASIMOV
WITH REVISIONS AND UPDATING BY FRANCIS REDDY

Gareth Stevens Publishing
MILWAUKEE

N

1860

For a free color catalog describing Gareth Stevens' list of high-quality books, call 1-800-542-2595 (USA) or 1-800-461-9120 (Canada). Gareth Stevens' Fax: (414) 225-0377.

A special thanks to Adolf Schaller.

Library of Congress Cataloging-in-Publication Data

Asimov, Isaac.
  Mysteries of deep space: black holes, pulsars, and quasars /
by Isaac Asimov and Francis Reddy.
      p. cm. — (Isaac Asimov's New library of the universe)
  Rev. ed. of: Quasars, pulsars, and black holes. 1988.
  Includes index.
  ISBN 0-8368-1133-X
  1. Cosmology—Juvenile literature. 2. Astronomy—Juvenile literature.
3. Stars – Juvenile literature. 4. Black holes (Astronomy)—Juvenile literature.
[1. Stars. 2. Galaxies. 3. Black holes (Astronomy) 4. Universe.] I. Reddy,
Francis, 1959-. II. Asimov, Isaac. Quasars, pulsars, and black holes. III. Title.
IV. Series: Asimov, Isaac. New library of the universe.
  QB983.A864   1994
  523.8—dc20   94-15429

J
523.8
ASI

This edition first published in 1994 by
Gareth Stevens Publishing
1555 North RiverCenter Drive, Suite 201
Milwaukee, Wisconsin 53212, USA

Project editor: Barbara J. Behm
Design adaptation: Helene Feider
Editorial assistant: Diane Laska
Production director: Susan Ashley
Picture research: Kathy Keller
Artwork commissioning: Kathy Keller and Laurie Shock

Printed in the United States of America

 2 3 4 5 6 7 8 9 9 99 98 97 96 95

To bring this classic of young people's information up to date, the editors at Gareth Stevens Publishing have selected two noted science authors, Greg Walz-Chojnacki and Francis Reddy. Walz-Chojnacki and Reddy coauthored the recent book *Celestial Delights: The Best Astronomical Events Through 2001.*

Walz-Chojnacki is also the author of the book *Comet: The Story Behind Halley's Comet* and various articles about the space program. He was an editor of *Odyssey,* an astronomy and space technology magazine for young people, for eleven years.

Reddy is the author of nine books, including *Halley's Comet, Children's Atlas of the Universe, Children's Atlas of Earth Through Time,* and *Children's Atlas of Native Americans,* plus numerous articles. He was an editor of *Astronomy* magazine for several years.

CONTENTS

We live in an enormously large place – the Universe. It's just in the last fifty-five years or so that we've found out how large it probably is. It's only natural that we would want to understand the place in which we live, so scientists have developed instruments – such as radio telescopes, satellites, probes, and many more – that have told us far more about the Universe than could possibly be imagined.

We have seen planets up close. We have learned about our Moon and the moons of other planets. We have gathered amazing data about how the Universe may have come into being and how it may end. Nothing could be more astonishing.

We have learned new things about the stars, too. Fifty-five years ago, the Universe seemed a quiet place. The stars seemed serene and unchanging. Now we know that stars can explode and leave behind bits of themselves that do incredible things. These bits are called neutron stars, or pulsars. We know that galaxies can have incredibly active centers, called quasars, and that there are black holes in space. Everything can fall into them, and nothing can escape!

Isaac Asimov

Unruly Stars

In the beginning, the Universe was filled with large clouds of dust and gas. Some of these clouds began to contract under their own gravitational pull. In each of these clouds, the matter packed together and increased in temperature. Finally, the matter became packed enough and hot enough to become a star. Our Sun formed this way nearly five billion years ago.

Stars still form out of clouds of dust and gas. One such cloud is the Orion Nebula, where astronomers can see small, dark, round spots. These are collapsing clouds that will eventually become shining stars.

Stars do not stay still. And they do not always behave themselves! Some twinkle, and some explode. Some collapse, and some collide with other stars. Some even swallow up light.

With its billions upon billions of stars, it is no wonder our Universe is such a fascinating place.

Top: The birth of the Sun began with the collapse of a cloud of gas and dust *(upper left)*. As the cloud contracted, the outer regions flattened into a disk *(center)*. The cloud's center erupted in a blaze, and the Sun was born *(right)*.

Bottom: A spectacular cloud of gases surrounds several hot stars deep inside the Orion Nebula. This cloud is visible to the naked eye as the middle star in the sword of the constellation Orion.

4

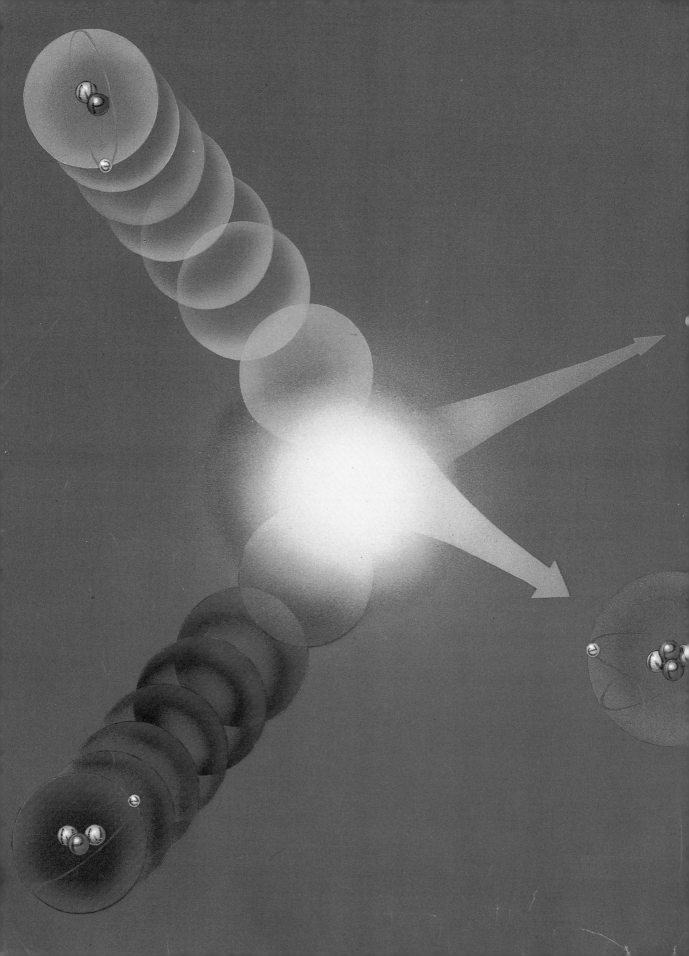

Shining Stars

Stars come in all sizes. Some are larger and brighter than the Sun. Some are smaller and dimmer. They are made mostly of hydrogen, the lightest element. Tiny particles of hydrogen smash together and form larger particles that make up the second lightest element, helium. This collision releases energy that keeps the stars shining.

The energy also keeps them from collapsing under their own gravitational pull. Large stars have more hydrogen to begin with, but their centers are hotter than the centers of small stars. So large stars burn their hydrogen more quickly than small stars.

Left: This illustration shows how fusion of hydrogen into helium might be performed on Earth to create energy. Two atoms of hydrogen in the form of deuterium *(upper left)* and tritium *(lower left)* actually have a bit more mass than the helium *(lower right)* and neutron *(upper right)* that are made by this process. A different form of fusion produces helium in the Sun to create sunshine.

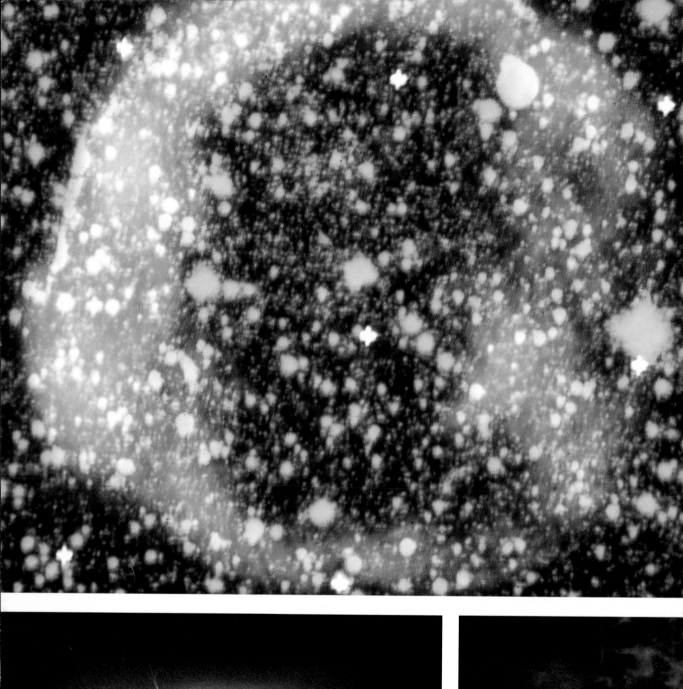

Blazes of Glory

As a star continues to shine, its center grows steadily hotter, and its hydrogen runs low. The extra heat makes it expand. Because of this expansion, the outer layers change to a cool red. The result is a red giant. As the red giant continues to shine, it finally runs out of energy at its center. Then it collapses.

This collapse is so rapid and violent that it creates an enormous explosion. This large, exploding star becomes a supernova. For a while, the explosion makes the supernova shine as brightly in the sky as an entire galaxy ordinarily does.

After such an explosion, matter flies into space or remains behind. The matter that remains behind will become a neutron star or a black hole.

Opposite, top: This ragged shell of gas is all that remains of a star that exploded tens of thousands of years ago.

Opposite, bottom, left: A black hole. What remains of a star after it explodes can be so dense that it may imprison even its own light. Although it may be called a hole, it is really an object of great mass. This illustration shows how the immense gravity of the dead star creates a deep well from which nothing can escape.

Below: From star to supernova – going out in a blaze of glory!

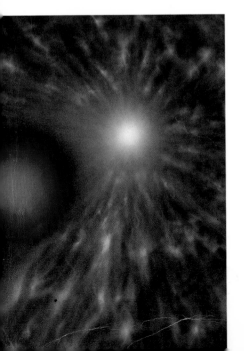

Small, but Mighty – the White Dwarf

When an ordinary star like the Sun collapses, its gravity squeezes it down to the size of a small planet. All the mass is there, but it has become a tiny, white-hot body called a white dwarf. If the mass of the Sun were squeezed into an object the size of Earth or less, a bit of the white-dwarf matter about the size of your little finger would weigh at least twenty tons. If the star is larger than the Sun to begin with, its greater gravity forces it together even more tightly. It becomes a neutron star, with all the mass of an ordinary star squeezed into a little ball perhaps 10 miles (16 km) across.

Below: These pictures show what is known as a double-star system. The larger star is a normal star. Its smaller companion is a neutron star. Around the neutron star is what is called an accretion disk. The disk is made up of matter from the normal star that has been sucked away by the neutron star's intense gravity. This matter forms the swirling disk and hits the surface of the neutron star at the center of the disk. The neutron star's gravity is so great that when matter hits the neutron star, a great deal of energy is released. For example, something as light as a marshmallow dropped on a neutron star would release energy equal to that of an atomic bomb.

Right: This illustration gives you an idea of what happens when a star collapses into a white dwarf or a neutron star. Imagine a twenty-ton cement mixer transforming into a cement mixer the size of your little finger and still weighing twenty tons!

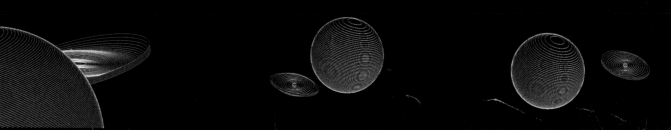

A neutron star — small matter, lots of mass!

Our Sun is too small to collapse into a neutron star. But what if it could? All its mass would be squeezed into a ball only 8 miles (13 km) across. The neutron star would take up only one-quadrillionth the space the Sun did. But a piece of its matter would weigh a quadrillion (1,000,000,000,000,000) times more than the same size piece of matter from the Sun. Suppose you made a ballpoint pen out of neutron star matter. A pen of ordinary matter might weigh .5 ounce (14 grams). But a pen of neutron star matter would weigh 15 billion tons!

Celestial Energy

In 1054, Chinese, Arab, and American Indian sky watchers looked up to the heavens and saw the result of a supernova that had exploded 6,500 light-years away from them. (One light-year is how far light travels in one year.) This supernova formed a huge, expanding cloud of dust and gas that we can still see. The cloud is called the Crab Nebula. At its center is a tiny neutron star, all that is left of the exploded star. This neutron star turns thirty-three times a second, sending a pulse of energy toward Earth with each turn. This energy is in the form of electromagnetic waves called radio waves. Scientists first noticed these pulses in the Crab Nebula in 1969 and began calling neutron stars *pulsars*. The Crab pulsar sends out pulses of light, too, blinking on and off thirty-three times a second.

Opposite: In 1054, astronomers saw a supernova, the Crab Nebula, whose "ashes" we see today as a cloud of hot gas. Today's technology can photograph the cloud to reveal its chemical parts. This photo shows hydrogen (red) and sulfur (blue) emissions from the nebula.

Inset: The hot inner regions of the Crab Nebula. The bright spot is the Crab pulsar. In one second, it blinks on and off thirty-three times. It is pictured here with its light on.

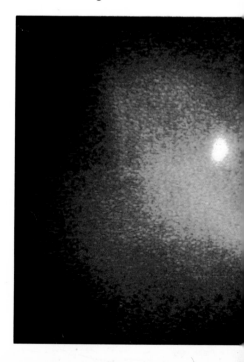

! Stars speaking from space!

In 1967, a young astronomy student, Jocelyn Bell, first detected the radio waves that flickered, or twinkled, rapidly from the sky. For a while, some people wondered if these waves were signals from beings in space. Scientists called them LGM, for Little Green Men. But the twinkles were so regular that scientists decided they couldn't be of intelligent origin. Bell had discovered pulsars – spinning neutron stars sending out radio waves with each turn.

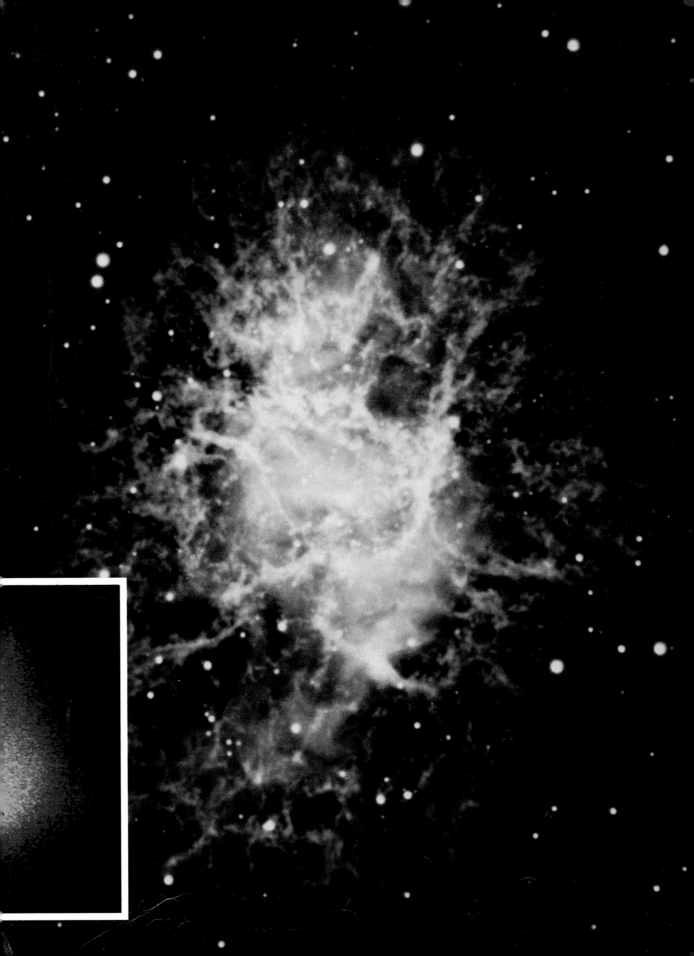

A Matter of Gravity

We know that gravity is a force that attracts objects to one another. But can you imagine what gravity actually looks like? Picture gravity by pretending space is a rubber sheet. Any heavy object resting on the sheet puts a dent in it. The heavier the object, the deeper the dent. If an object is kept heavy but is made smaller, the weight is concentrated on a smaller area, and the dent gets deeper. A white dwarf makes a much deeper dent than Earth does. A neutron star makes a still deeper dent. The deeper the dent, the harder it would be for an object to escape if it fell in. What if something is so small and heavy that it forms a dent too deep for anything to escape – ever?

! *Pulsars – you can set your watch by them.*

Pulsars turn so steadily in the sky that they could be used as nearly perfect clocks. In fact, pulsars have been used to chart Earth's position in the Galaxy. On board the Pioneer 10 *and* 11 *space probes are plaques containing information about the location of Earth. Pulsars are included in maps on these plaques. Scientists know that the rates at which these pulsars turn would change very little in the time it might take for the plaques to be discovered by other beings in space – perhaps millions of years. So these maps would help extraterrestrial beings locate Earth from anywhere in the Galaxy.*

Left: This diagram shows the pull of the gravitational fields on three objects: *(left to right)* the Sun, a neutron star, and a black hole. See how the large Sun barely distorts the grid. The smaller neutron star distorts the grid somewhat with its more concentrated mass. The smallest object – the black hole – distorts the grid lines most of all due to its tremendous gravitational pull.

No Way Out – Black Holes

It is hard to fight the gravity of small objects packed tightly with matter. For example, the gravity of a neutron star is almost impossible for an object to escape. Only fast-moving gas and electromagnetic radiation – such as light, heat, and radio waves – can succeed. And if a star could be made even more compact, *nothing* could leave its surface. Not even light! If everything fell in and nothing came out, this would be similar to a hole in space. Since even light cannot escape, astronomers call such an object a black hole. When a large star explodes, it leaves behind an inner core that can become a neutron star. But if the core contains more than three times the mass of our Sun, it can be squeezed into a black hole.

Opposite: The most massive black holes may not be associated with the death of stars, but with the centers of galaxies. Astronomers think this is what the central depths of some galaxies may look like – a central black hole draws stars, gas, and dust into an enormous disk. Some of this material is not absorbed by the black hole, but instead forms jets that stretch far into space.

Below: A jet of gas extends 5,000 light-years from the core of the giant galaxy called M87. The bright hot spot at the galaxy's center is believed to be caused by gas falling into an enormous black hole.

! Double pulsars — a recipe for trouble?

Astronomers have found cases where two pulsars are close and circling each other. All the while, they are giving off radiation and losing energy. This causes them to get slightly closer to each other with every turn. Eventually, they will collide. What will happen when two pulsars collide? The mass will double. The mass might grow so large that additional gravity will cause it to collapse into a black hole.

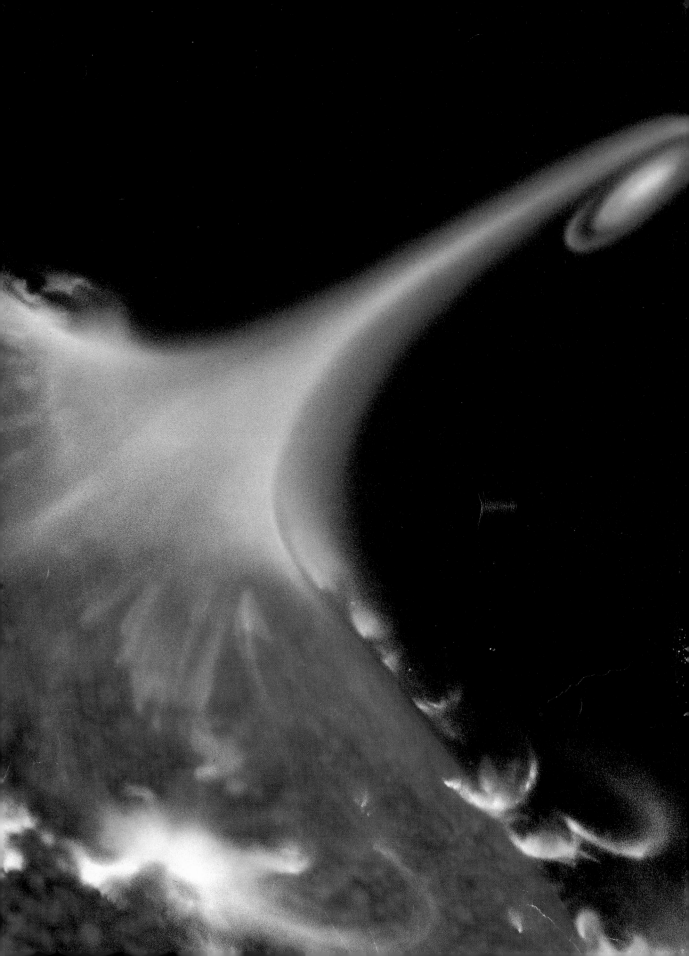

The Search for Black Holes

If even light cannot escape a black hole, how can scientists find them? The only way to identify a black hole is through its interactions with other matter astronomers can see. If the black hole orbits a star, for example, some of the star's gas may flow into the black hole. As gas falls toward the hole, it swirls into a flattened disk. Its molecules move ever faster, bunching up and colliding. This makes the gas very hot – so hot that it gives off X rays! Although we can't see the black hole, satellites can detect X rays. The first black hole to be confirmed was found in the core of the giant galaxy M87 in 1994. In addition, a good candidate for a black hole is an X-ray source that circles an orange star in the constellation Monoceros. Another possible black hole orbits a giant blue star in the constellation Cygnus.

? Mini-black holes: a mega-problem?

A scientist, Stephen Hawking, has shown that black holes can very slowly evaporate and turn into thin gas. The smaller they are, the more quickly they evaporate. When the Universe began, perhaps black holes of all sizes were formed. Some might have been mini-black holes, having about the same mass as planets or even asteroids. These may be scattered throughout space, and scientists would only be able to detect them if the black holes are close enough to Earth. What would happen to Earth if a mini-black hole approached our Solar System? Scientists do not know.

Left: The small, flat, spiral disk *(upper right)* shows that a black hole is stealing matter from its neighboring star. X rays given off by the whirling matter tell us a black hole exists here, although the black hole itself is invisible.

A Black Hole Reality

Astronomers have found a great deal of energy coming from the centers of many galaxies. For a long time, scientists thought there were enormous black holes lying in the middle of these galaxies. In 1994, astronomers were using the Hubble Space Telescope to look at the center of M-87, a galaxy in the constellation Virgo, 50 million light-years away. In the core of the giant galaxy, they found the signs of an extraordinarily powerful black hole that has the mass of three billion Suns!

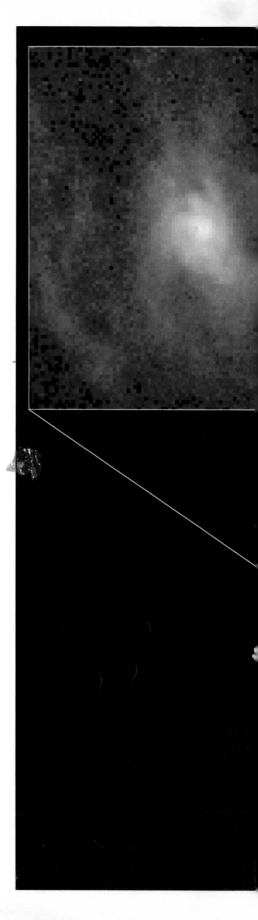

Opposite: M-87 is a galaxy with an enormous jet shooting from its heart. The Hubble Space Telescope was able to peer into the galaxy's heart and see a disk *(inset)*. Measurements of the disk showed it was spinning at a rate of over one million miles (1,609,000 km) per hour. Only the gravity of a black hole could keep such speedy material in orbit. Astronomers found that although the black hole weighs as much as three billion Suns, it is concentrated into a space smaller than our Solar System.

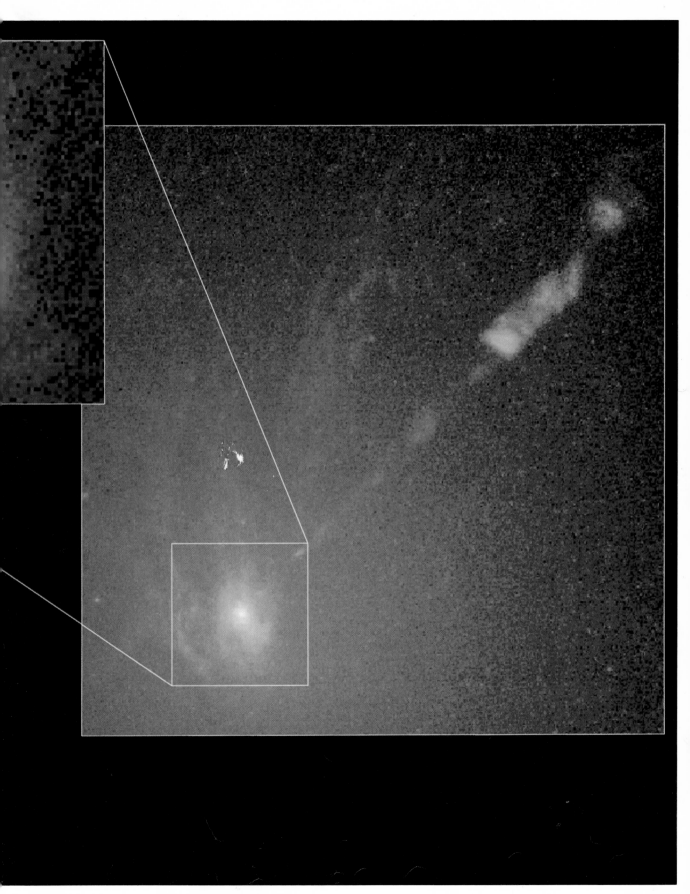

The Bright Light of Quasars

The Universe is full of objects that fascinate and puzzle us. In the past, one such group of objects looked like faint stars. At first, in the late 1950s, astronomers thought these objects were ordinary stars of our own Galaxy – except that they gave off radio waves. But then astronomers watched them more closely and studied their light. By 1963, it was determined that these objects were anywhere from 1 billion to 10 billion light-years away. Astronomers soon found many more of these "stars" that were not radio sources but were just as distant. And as recently as 1987, British and American astronomers detected an object that may be 12 billion light-years away. These objects are galaxies so far off they wouldn't normally be seen except that their centers are unusually bright – a hundred times brighter than ordinary galactic centers. These extra-bright centers are called quasars.

The word *quasar* comes from two words, *quasi* and *stellar*. Together, these two words mean "starlike." What makes quasars bright may be the presence of large black holes at their centers. These black holes would draw in all sorts of glowing stellar matter, from stars to dust.

Below: A quasar interacts with a nearby galaxy, drawing in matter to the quasar's center.

Opposite: If we could see to the edge of the Universe, might we find newly formed galaxies, like this spiral, with a quasar as its center?

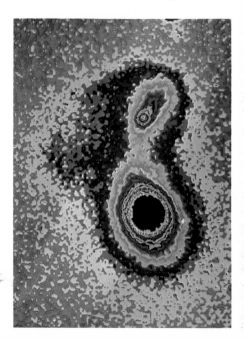

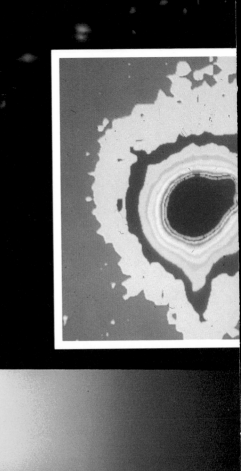

The Red Shift

Opposite: The red shift at a glance. A galaxy's hydrogen atoms can emit blue light, as seen in the galaxy pictured *(on the left)*. However, that same light will appear redder and redder *(on the right)* as we look at galaxies located farther from Earth. The colors of the spectrum *(opposite, bottom)* also show a greater shift toward the red end of the spectrum as the galaxies move farther away from Earth.

Inset: In this computer-enhanced image, a quasar *(left)* seems to be interacting with a galaxy *(right)*. The big question: Are the two actually attached? Most astronomers believe the quasar is actually many times farther away from us than the galaxy.

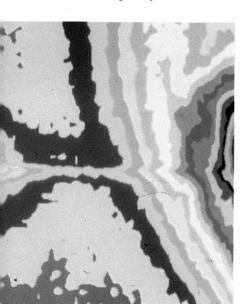

How can we tell that quasars are so far away? Because certain scientific instruments can spread the light from any star into what is known as a spectrum, or rainbow, of colors – red, orange, yellow, green, blue, indigo, and violet. Dark lines are across the rainbow. When an object that gives off light moves away from Earth, the dark lines move, or shift, toward the red end of the spectrum. The faster the object travels, the farther the shift toward red. Since the Universe is expanding, distant objects are all moving away and show this red shift. The greater the red shift, the farther away they are.

When quasars were first discovered, they showed a greater red shift than any other known object. That is why scientists felt that quasars were the farthest known objects in the Universe. But in 1988, astronomers from the University of Arizona announced they had detected objects that might be even farther away – and older – than any known quasar. These objects might be as far as 17 billion light-years away! Scientists think the objects might be primeval galaxies, galaxies in their very earliest stages of development.

Top: The Milky Way and Andromeda galaxies – will they collide? Or will they just slide through each other? New evidence suggests that our neighboring galaxy may have swallowed up a smaller galaxy.

Right: In this false-color picture, the center of our Galaxy, the Milky Way, emits radio waves produced by hot gas. The red area is where the gas is most dense.

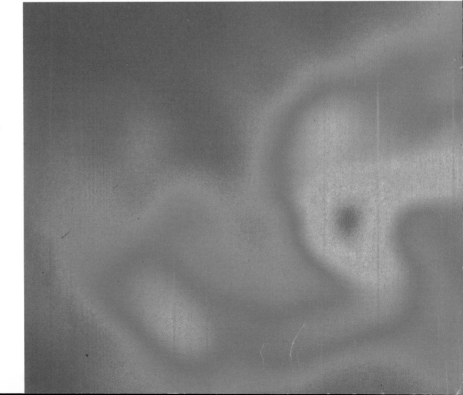

Was Our Galaxy Once a Quasar?

When we see a quasar that is 12 billion light-years away, we know that the light from this quasar took 12 billion years to reach Earth. This means we see the quasar as it was 12 billion years ago. This would be when it and the Universe – which we think is 15-20 billion years old – were very young. So the fact that quasars are so far away may mean that young galaxies – which shine very brightly – are more likely to be quasars than old ones. Perhaps our own Milky Way Galaxy was a quasar billions of years ago, but then it settled down. If so, that's a good thing. A galactic center burning as brightly as a quasar would fill the galaxy with so much energy that it might not be possible for life to develop in it.

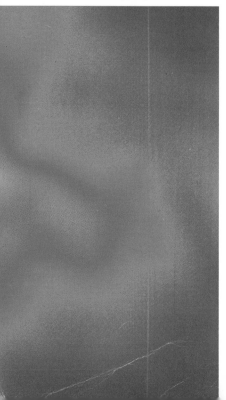

? *Close encounters of the galactic kind – a future crack-up?*

Our Milky Way and the Andromeda galaxies move around in the same cluster. Sometimes we are farther apart, and sometimes we are closer together. Recently, a scientist found evidence that the two galaxies will collide in about four billion years. Imagine these two colossal star systems – each containing hundreds of billions of stars – smacking into each other!

However, there is a great deal of room between the stars in each galaxy and few, if any, stars would actually collide. The galaxies would just slide through each other. But the galaxies would be shaken by gravity, and our own Sun could go spinning off, leaving its home galaxy forever. But don't worry just yet – four billion years is a long time from now!

Fact File: Quasar, the Prize for Power

A

Quasars – what we can see of them comes to us from distances so vast that we can barely imagine how far away, and how long ago, they existed. Some are believed to be 12 billion light-years away. For years, astronomers thought they were the oldest visible objects in the Universe. Astronomers now believe they have discovered objects in space that could be as distant as 17 billion light-years away. These are primeval galaxies. We see them as they were in the earliest stages of their creation, before the Universe was old enough to spawn quasars. But quasars still win the prize for power. The majority of astronomers believe quasars are the most powerful energy sources in the sky.

On the opposite page are two pictures. Picture A is of a spiral galaxy with a quasar at its core. Picture B gives us a close-up look at the core, showing the black hole that may lie at the heart of the quasar.

Picture A

Subject:
- A violent spiral galaxy deep in the cosmos.

Special features:
- High-energy quasar at galactic core.
- Black hole at center.
- Accretion disk — a gravitational whirlpool of hot gas in a ring around the center feeding the black hole and the quasar.
- Gas jets spewing excess particles at right angles to disk.

Picture B

Subject:
- A detailed view of the galactic core, showing the quasar and its black hole center.

Special features:
- Sideways view of accretion disk. The disk might stretch out to a diameter one hundred times that of our Solar System.
- Black hole at center of disk. Because of huge amount of stellar matter swirling around the center, the black hole would not normally be visible. A black hole like this might have the mass of billions of stars the size of our Sun jammed into a space no bigger than that of our Solar System.
- Jets shooting matter at a right angle to the accretion disk. This is matter that is in excess of what the black hole can absorb. The matter shoots out to distances that could approach millions of light-years. This would be farther than the distance between our Milky Way and its nearest galactic neighbor, the Andromeda Galaxy.

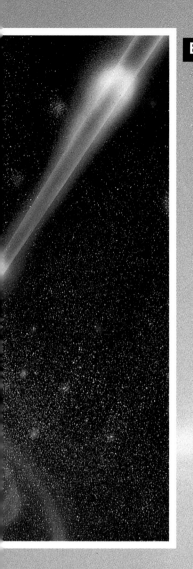

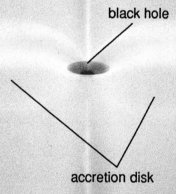

B

gas jet

black hole

accretion disk

More Books about Black Holes, Pulsars, and Quasars

Bright Stars, Red Giants, and White Dwarfs. Berger (Putnam)
Our Vast Home: The Milky Way. Asimov (Gareth Stevens)
Stars. Simon (Morrow)
The Stars: From Birth to Black Hole. Darling (Dillon)
Sun and Stars. Barrett (Franklin Watts)

Video

The Sun. (Gareth Stevens)

Places to Visit

You can explore black holes, pulsars, quasars, and other parts of the Universe without leaving Earth. Here are some museums and centers where you can find a variety of space exhibits.

NASA Lewis Research Center
Educational Services Office
21000 Brookpark Road
Cleveland, OH 44135

NASA Goddard Space Flight Center
Greenbelt Road
Greenbelt, MD 20771

Perth Observatory
Walnut Road
Bickley, W.A. 6076 Australia

Henry Crown Science Center
Museum of Science and Industry
57th Street and Lake Shore Drive
Chicago, IL 60637

Edmonton Space and Science Centre
11211 - 142nd Street
Edmonton, Alberta K5M 4A1

Ontario Science Centre
770 Don Mills Road
Don Mills, Ontario M3C 1T3

Places to Write

Here are some places you can write for more information about black holes, pulsars, and quasars. Be sure to state what kind of information you would like. Include your full name and address so they can write back to you.

Jet Propulsion Laboratory
Public Affairs 180-201
4800 Oak Grove Drive
Pasadena, CA 91109

Sydney Observatory
P.O. Box K346
Haymarket 2000
Australia

Department of Industry
235 Queen Street
Ottawa, Ontario K1A 0H5

For photographs of stars and galaxies:
Caltech Bookstore
California Institute of Technology
Mail Code 1-51
Pasadena, CA 91125

Glossary

billion: the number represented by 1 followed by nine zeroes – 1,000,000,000. In some countries, this number is called "a thousand million." In these countries, one billion would then be represented by 1 followed by twelve zeroes – 1,000,000,000,000 – a million million.

black hole: a burned-out star, its mass so dense and tightly packed that not even light can escape the force of its gravity.

Crab Nebula: a huge expanding cloud of dust and gas that is visible from Earth. It was first reported in 1054 and is the result of a supernova.

fusion: the joining of hydrogen atoms under extreme heat. Helium is formed, and the energy released during this process is what makes stars shine.

galaxy: any of the many large groupings of stars, gas, and dust that exists in the Universe.

helium: a light, colorless gas that makes up part of every star.

hydrogen: a colorless, odorless gas that is the simplest and lightest of the elements. Stars are three-quarters hydrogen.

light-year: the distance light travels in one year – nearly 6 trillion miles (9.5 trillion km).

Milky Way: the name of our Galaxy.

NASA: the space agency in the United States – the National Aeronautics and Space Administration.

neutron star: a collapsed star, the leftover core of a supernova.

Orion Nebula: one of the huge clouds of dust and gas in which stars are forming.

pulsar: a neutron star that sends out rapid pulses of light or electrical waves.

quasar: a starlike core of a galaxy that may have a large black hole at its center.

radio telescope: an instrument that uses a radio receiver and antenna both to see into space and listen for messages from space.

red giants: huge stars that develop when their hydrogen runs low and the extra heat makes them expand. Their outer layers then change to a cool red.

Solar System: our Planetary System – the Sun, planets, and all other bodies that orbit the Sun.

supernova: a red giant that has collapsed, heating its cool outer layers and causing explosions.

Universe: everything we know that exists and believe may exist.

white dwarf: the small, white-hot body that remains when a star like our Sun collapses.

Index

Born in 1920, Isaac Asimov came to the United States as a young boy from his native Russia. As a young man, he was a student of biochemistry. In time, he became one of the most productive writers the world has ever known. His books cover a spectrum of topics, including science, history, language theory, fantasy, and science fiction. His brilliant imagination gained him the respect and admiration of adults and children alike. Sadly, Isaac Asimov died shortly after the publication of the first edition of *Isaac Asimov's Library of the Universe*.

The publishers wish to thank the following for permission to reproduce copyright material: front cover, pp. 4-5 (upper), © Mark Paternostro 1988; 4-5 (lower), National Optical Astronomy Observatories; 6-7, © Sally Bensusen 1987; 8 (upper), National Optical Astronomy Observatories; 8 (lower), 8-9, © Mark Paternostro 1988; 10-11 (upper), © Lynette Cook 1988; 10-11 (lower), Courtesy of William Priedhorsky, Los Alamos National Laboratory; 12-13, Smithsonian Institution; 13, The Crab Nebula, Messier 1, From plates of the Hale 5m telescope, © Malin/Pasachoff/Caltech 1992; 14-15, © Julian Baum 1988; 16, Tod R. Lauer and Sandra M. Faber/NASA; 17, 18-19, © Mark Paternostro 1988; 20-21, Holland Ford/NASA; 22, National Optical Astronomy Observatories; 23, © Mark Paternostro 1988; 24, © Adolf Schaller 1988; 24-25, National Optical Astronomy Observatories; 26-27 (upper), © Mark Paternostro 1983; 26-27 (lower), National Radio Astronomy Observatory; 28-29, © Michael Carroll 1987; 29, © Mark Paternostro 1988.